www.**transworldbooks**.co.uk

# WTF Knits

GABRIELLE GRILLO

and LUCY SWEET

BANTAM PRESS

LONDON · TORONTO · SYDNEY · AUCKLAND · JOHANNESBURG

TRANSWORLD PUBLISHERS
61–63 Uxbridge Road, London W5 5SA
A Random House Group Company
www.transworldbooks.co.uk

First published in Great Britain
in 2014 by Bantam Press
an imprint of Transworld Publishers

A CIP catalogue record for this book
is available from the British Library.

ISBN 9780593074442

Addresses for Random House Group Ltd companies outside the UK
can be found at: www.randomhouse.co.uk
The Random House Group Ltd Reg. No. 954009

Typeset in Hand of Sean and Trade Gothic
Printed and bound in China
2 4 6 8 10 9 7 5 3 1

To everyone who has sent me such bad-taste photos to fuel my blog, and especially to Goran, my dear friend, and the person who has been my most prolific image provider.

# Introduction

How did *WTF Knits* begin? Well, if you go to the last (or first, depending on how you look at it) page of the Fucked Up Knitting Tumblr, you'll see a hilarious picture of a giant sock monkey with a huge penis, sharing the frame with a cute, smiling blonde girl. There's a date attached to the post: 9 March. I'm not even sure what year it was. And below the photograph, there's a very simple caption that says: via @filleauxcraies.

That day, some random person on Twitter shared a picture she'd stumbled upon, and I thought 'OMG, I can't let that go.' So I signed up on Tumblr and posted the image along with the caption. Back then, I didn't know it would be the beginning of an odd collection that was going to make me, and lots of other people who started to follow the blog, laugh our pants off in a very bewildered way.

And now the blog has become a book — full of weird, wonderful and extremely fucked-up knitting and crochet from around the globe. From burgers and unicorns to a delightful toilet roll and cheery-looking poo, it seems there's no end to the craziness you can create with a pair of knitting needles or a crochet hook.

Some people make twisted worlds in wool — scenes from horror movies, roadkill, or freaky serial-killer clown masks. Others merrily wrap themselves in knitted prawn scarves and wear knitted raw chicken on their heads. As you flick through the book, the only question on your lips will be: 'WTF WERE THEY THINKING?' (Especially when you see the woman puking up woolly vomit in a forest on page 34.)

But while you're laughing, it's important to remember that although these pictures of boob cushions or crocheted turds are funny, someone, somewhere, worked hard to craft them – whether it was for fun, or to make a work of art. These pieces might be baffling, but they're original and they're made with love.

So I want to say thank you to all the people who have created these amazingly weird knits and allowed us to publish their photos. And I also want to pay homage to them, because I think the world is a more creative and interesting place filled with tortoise cosies, weird balaclavas and Princess Leia hats.

As for the girl who posted that first image on Twitter – sadly, she's no longer with us. She'll never know that this crazy book exists because of her post. Or that the royalties that come from it will go to a charity that supports research into the disease that took her.

But I'm sure she'd agree that a book which features cats in shark hats and dogs with dreadlocks is no place for sadness. Instead, dip into it at your leisure, find your favourite photo and yell out 'WTF?' And let's all get inspired to start knitting, crocheting and yarnbombing the world – one (well-endowed) sock monkey at a time!

## Gabrielle Grillo
fuckedupknitting.tumblr.com

God knows what 'possessed' them to crochet
The Exorcist, but it's one hell of a yarn.

Mmmm! A takeaway burger
and fries, made from
delicious 100% wool. OK, so
it might make your mouth
a bit dry, but who cares?
You're drunk!

Sorry, Fido. Hugh Hefner isn't going to make you a Playboy Bunny until you get a wax.

You've heard of the Red Room of Pain? Well, welcome to the Pink Room of Fluff! Just out of shot, there's a granny with a very open mind.

13

'Eat your dinner, darling! It's BRAIN FOOD!'

Although enterprising, this hat is highly illogical, Captain.

The elephant thong is the perfect way to emasculate your boyfriend. It's cute, though, isn't it?

Don't you just hate talented, successful people with their fingers in many pies?

Holy guacamole, these avocados taste weird.

Here's a phallic cymbal that will haunt you for ever. Next time you close your eyes, the only thing you'll see is a big pair of woolly monkey nuts . . .

Try getting to sleep tonight with this photo in the house. JUST TRY.

Forget Wolf of Wall Street, Dallas Buyers Club or True Detective . . .

. . . Matthew McConaughey's role as Weird Naked Bongo Dude might turn out to be his most challenging yet.

'Darling, we need to talk. This bank robbery is going really badly. In fact, I think it's all been an elaborate ploy to stick your tongue down my throat.'

23

Mr Hankey the Christmas Poo is a festive addition to any dinner table. And with this handy knitted version, year after year he will never smear.

Meet Sister Mary and Sister Assumpta.
They're the holy nunchucks, with a black belt
in Jesus-Jitsu, ready to deliver you from evil.

With this large knitted mammary gland you can
make a complete tit of yourself any time of day.

'Hi, is that the psychiatrist? I've knitted a scarf made of salad. Can you help me get back on the straight and marrow – I mean, narrow?'

27

Monkey see, donkey do. How this genetically modified mondonkey goes to the bathroom, or has any privacy at all, is anyone's guess.

The Queen will never notice if you steal the Crown Jewels and replace them with this. Even the rubies look real!

'Where did I put my tights? I'm sure they were around here somewhere. Honestly, I'd forget my head if I weren't wearing it.'

31

In a galaxy far, far away, this is fashionable.

Make a terrifying fashion statement with this arresting clown serial-killer cape, crocheted entirely from spaghetti.

33

When you have too many drinks, a bag of frozen peas and some marshmallows, this is what happens.

Feeling peckish? Just pop the dissected alien baby on a baking tray, put it in the oven for 20 minutes, and you'll have a tasty snack that's out of this world!

Never lock yourself out of the bathroom again with this handy and attractive poo-ring. Take it to the pub with your mates and it'll talk shite for hours.

Knitrex woolly toilet roll is very strong, and very, very long. In fact, it lasts for ages! You can also wear it as a scarf – but you should probably wash it first.

Nobody will ever notice you in this outfit. With all this clever camouflage, you'll easily be able to slip through the undergrowth undetected. IF YOU'RE AT AN ACID MONKEY RAVE ON THE MOON, that is.

Even the jumper looks horrified.

Is this dog supposed to be Medusa, or has he started his own reggae tribute band, Dog Marley and the Woofers? Either way, get the scissors.

When you light a Woolboro, all your cares go up in smoke. And your eyebrows, your hair, your house . . .

She's probably annoyed that she can't have a drink,
thanks to the fact that there isn't a mouth hole.

YOU'RE POKING OUT, LOVE. If Janet Jackson
can't get away with a nipple malfunction at
the Superbowl, neither can you . . .

43

This recreation of the tragic argument between Sid Vicious and Nancy Spungen in the Chelsea Hotel in 1978 is uncannily accurate. There are only two things missing. Her feet.

'I dunno, pal. Something tells me this guy isn't the real Santa Claus.'

45

This cosy chainsaw scarf will keep you warm and make you look great all winter, unless you press that black button!

Prawnography is a tricky career for anyone, but Marie Rose was sure that it would work out . . .

I SEAFOOD and EAT IT! Actually, can I SEA the dessert menu? I'm starting to feel a little bit sick . . .

For rent: a friendly uterus share in the heart of Wombton – roomy, flexible space, ideal for a very young person, close to Fallopian tube station, lease 9 months. (NO SMOKERS, PLEASE.)

Talk about making an ass of yourself,
you so-called three wise monkeys.

Don't know about you, but I always like to measure my knitted poo to make sure it fits the European Faeces Standard. At 2 ½ inches wide, this one qualifies to enter the coveted Caca D'Or award for length, breadth and texture. Poo la la!

For just a small donation each month, you could help this dog realize his dream of being a unicorn. Please call today to give what you can.

You know the expression 'wearing your heart on your sleeve'? Well, with this fetching knitted onesie, you can also wear your colon on your arse.

53

Does anybody know what this is?
A pencil case? A tail-less squirrel?
Totoro? Whatever it is, it needs a bucket.

Whoever made this needs a brain scan.

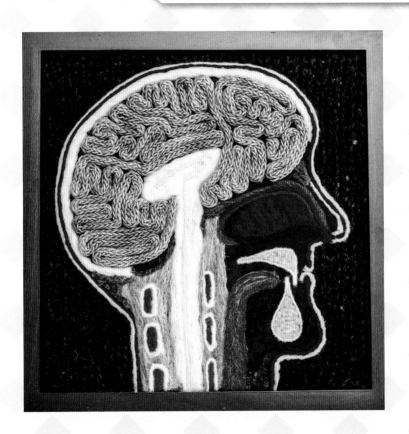

Just before he croaked, he donated his body to science.

Well, we all have bad hair days, but this seems like a pretty drastic solution.

Despite coming 780,323rd in the London Marathon,
Freda the tortoise thought she looked pretty dashing.

Is it weird that the knitted versions - with the vagina triangle chestwigs - are actually more attractive than the real Bee Gees?

Take a butcher's at this display – it looks beautiful, but chances are it tastes offal.

PÂTE FORESTIER

Andouille de Guémené

'I look like a nice fluffy kitteh, but I am a BEEEEG vicious predator, capable of killing yew with one devastating bite of mah JAWS!! Oooh, look – a saucer of milk! Laterz!'

Today on PlentyofFish.com: Clawdia, 22, would like to meet crustacean male, 25-30, for good times.

Must have GSOH, and not be shellfish or crabby.

Teddy didn't believe in unicorns.
HE DOES NOW.

Thinking of going vegan . . . ?

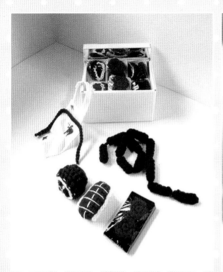

You are now.

65

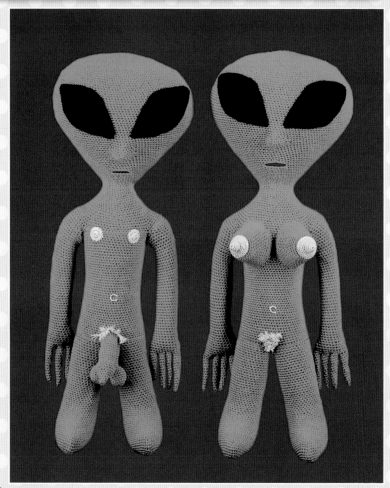

Uh-oh. William Tell should have gone to Specsavers.

Life is full of unanswered questions. Like: is there life on other planets? Why is Peter Andre famous? And what the hell is this?

When people say
'Nature is cruel,'
this is what they
mean. *shudder*

Awww, bless. This baby got the booby prize.

Poor Carrie the crocheted teddy bear. The bucket of pig's blood and the humiliation at the prom was enough to make a girl completely unravel.

71

Karl Lagerfeld always likes to wind down after an exhausting Paris Fashion Week by having a little lie down in the rug department at Ikea.

Oh yeah,
he's bad,
he's bad,
you know it.

73

Do you sit on this, or report it to the police for sexual harassment?

The bikini doesn't look very waterproof,
but at least she's nicely bronzed.

It's very colourful, but the new Nando's uniform seems a tad impractical, to be honest. Surely you'd get peri peri sauce all over your frilly bits?

That's the last time this pigeon will leave a
'lucky' deposit on someone's shoulder.

Ever done such a handsome poo that you feel you deserve an award? Well here it is, you high achiever, you.

POO AWARD

All hail the poo fairy – reliever of the constipated, harbinger of smells, blocker of the toilet. When you get wind of her, you'll be putting a pound under HER pillow just to make her go away.

Feeling a bit flushed?

What's this? Donald Trump's wig? A prolapsed sheep? Ah, it's a sperm fertilizing an egg! Jesus, if this were what the human reproductive process actually looked like, the human race would have died out centuries ago.

Awww! Look at the guillotine's funny little face! And check out the executioner's nipples! Never has being sentenced to death by decapitation been so cuddly.

Meanwhile, at the graveyarn . . . 'HELP! Let me live again! I never got to go to the John Lewis haberdashery department and meet a nice Rowan wool mix with added angora!'

Gonzo from the Muppets has never been the same since he got that eye infection.

Can't decide if it's a wasp's nest or a Gene Simmons from Kiss tribute act.

Somebody take this dog to the vet - now.

My First Game
of Thrones Doll
(dragons not included)

87

This handmade ravenous crocodile is a
lovely cuddly companion, and sure to
become a favourite at bedtime. Perfect
for a soon-to-be-traumatized kid.
(A lifetime of therapy not included.)

We've heard of 'slow food', but this is RIDICULOUS.

Introducing the new tort(oise)-illa, from Taco Shell.

Nothing says 'Oh shit, I forgot to defrost the turkey' like this lovely hat. Wear this, pop yourself in the oven at Gas Mark 5, and wait until your head crisps up (or bursts into flames). Voilà dinner!

'Hiiiii-yaaaargh!' Uh-oh. Looks like Kermit finally snapped.

92

Ah, so this is why
they call heroin
'horse'. Just say
neigh, Dobbin.
Just say neigh.

There's nothing like a delicious steak! And this is NOTHING like a delicious steak. In fact, it's more like a sanitary pad - a sanitary pad that will float for ever in the toilet bowl of hell.

Originally there were five-a-day, but the shady-looking aubergine chopped up the courgette and buried it under the patio.

This is the real reason that herbal tea tastes like crap.

They're Hershey's Kisses, aren't they?
Yes, let's just say they're Hershey's
Kisses, and ignore the funny smell.

97

It might look messy, but Death by Carrot is actually the rabbit's preferred way to die, along with Smothering by Lettuce.

In retrospect, it was probably a mistake to ask Quentin Tarantino to direct *Peter Rabbit: The Movie*.

You know that episode of *Friends* when Joey gets the
Thanksgiving turkey stuck on his head? Well, basically, if
you buy this hat, you can look like that ALL THE TIME.

You are cordially invited to the ChamberPot Gallery reception June 20 6pm

"Fecal Matters" brought to you by jafagirlart.com

Honestly, these farty types. Always showing off and trying to flog their log. Actually, Saatchi will probably buy this for millions and one day people will flock to see it at the Poo-uvre in Paris. (Sorry.)

She loved her fry-up so much, she decided to make a jacket out of it.

When you've knitted yourself a
beard of bees and a hat that looks
like a spinach omelette, it's time to
put down the needles, love.

103

'Darling, you bought crunchy embryos!
You know I only like the smooth kind.'

'Mmmm, that looks lovely. Shall we get a takeaway?'

Still a more convincing
Batman than Ben Affleck.

Shelly always had a bee in her bonnet about something.

Here's Bradley the Big Poo. He's a bit sensitive about his size since he was bullied as a child about his weight, but he's taking self-confidence-boosting seminars to improve his body image. Go, Bradley! One day, nobody will be able to flush you away.

We all make mistakes, so why not celebrate them with Timmy the Broken Condom Baby Hat?

# Picture Acknowledgements

## The authors are grateful to the following for the use of their photos:

10: Shove Mink,
www.croshame.com
11: Kate Jenkins, www.cardigan.ltd.uk
12: Hiroko Fukatsu
13: Patricia Waller,
www.patriciawaller.com
14: Daniela Edburg, 'Breakfast With Brain'
2011, www.danielaedburg.com
15: Daniela Edburg,
'Breakfast With Breasts' 2011,
www.danielaedburg.com
16: Rebecca Stundel,
www.etsy.com/fr/shop/FiveCornersDesign
17: Design of Alyona Pakhomova,
www.AlpachHandMade.etsy.com
18: Annette Morrison,
www.cheewawamommadesigns.com
19: Ashley Gerst,
www.ashleygerst.com
20: Monika Lidman, photograph © John
Kieltyka, www.verkstad.com
21: Katie Freeman,
www.etsy.com/shop/Knitrocious
22: Alison Hoffman,
www.craftyiscool.com, CraftyisCool on
Facebook/@craftyiscool on Twitter
23: Andrea Vander Kooij, 2006;
photographer: Kate Fellerath
24-25: Annette Morrison,
www.cheewawamommadesigns.com
26: Ansley Bleu,
www.ansleybleu.etsy.com
27: Ashley Gerst,
www.ashleygerst.com
28: Cannelle Delieutraz,
www.rockmylaine.com
29-30: Carissa Browning,

www.carissaknits.com
31: Photographer: Kurt Vandevelde,
Caroline Bosmans
www.carolinebosmans.com
32: Ansley Bleu,
www.ansleybleu.etsy.com
33: Aldo Lanzini, 'Dust Yourself Off And Try
Again' www.aldolanzini.eu
34: Daniela Edburg, 'Vomit' 2008,
www.danielaedburg.com
35: Emily Stoneking,
www.northatlanticyarn.bigcartel.com /
www.aknitomy.etsy.com
36-37: Emmanuelle Esther,
www.emmanuelle-esther.com / www.c-f-t.net
38-39: Hannah Taylor, www.hanzipan.co.uk
40: Hiroko Fukatsu
41: Kate Jenkins www.cardiganltd.uk
42-43: Aldo Lanzini, 'I Like the Universe';
'Sophia Lamar' www.aldolanzini.eu
44: Shove Mink, www.croshame.com
45: Paul Croes – Behind Eyes – Animal
Photography in studio,
www.facebook.com/paul.croes
46: Annette Morrison,
www.cheewawamommadesigns.com
47-48: Ashley Gerst,
www.ashleygerst.com
49-51: Carissa Browning,
www.carissaknits.com
52: Hiroko Fukatsu
53: Photographer: Kurt Vandevelde,
Caroline Bosmans
www.carolinebosmans.com
54: Elena Ho,
www.flickr.com/photos/elenaho
55-56: Emily Stoneking,

www.northatlanticyarn.bigcartel.com /
www.aknitomy.etsy.com
57: Katie Boyette
58: Katie Bradley,
www.etsy.com/shop/MossyTortoise
59: Lisa Balman
60: Madame Tricot, www.madametricot.ch,
photographer: Martin Graf
61: Mizuha Iizuka, blog.pokkeboy.com
62: Nanae Ito,
www.iheartamicute.blogspot.fr
63: Patricia Waller, www.patriciawaller.com
64-65: Nanae Ito,
www.iheartamicute.blogspot.fr
66-68: Patricia Waller,
www.patriciawaller.com
69: Phoenixknits,
www.ravelry.com/stores/phoenixknits
70: Sharon Coleman,
www.knittingabacus.com
71: Shove Mink, www.croshame.com
72-75: Solène Lebon-Couturier, Collectif
France Tricot, www.c-f-t.net
76: Aldo Lanzini, 'If you still complain you'll
meet an army of me' www.aldolanzini.eu
77: Emily Stoneking,
www.northatlanticyarn.bigcartel.com /
www.aknitomy.etsy.com
78-79: Corrine Bayraktaroglu,
www.jafabrit.blogspot.com;
photographer: Beth Clarke Lerman
80: Katie Boyette
81: Towe My Frykenfeldht,
www.flickr.com/photos/towemy
82-83: Shove Mink, www.croshame.com
84-85: Aldo Lanzini, 'The eyes are there

where they see, the things are there where
they are seen'; 'You can live or you can die,
ain't no time to wonder why'
www.aldolanzini.eu
86: Emmanuelle Esther,
www.emmanuelle-esther.com / www.c-f-t.net
87: Isabel Berglund, 'Woman's chair Uden
Skrift' www.isabelberglund.dk,
photographer: Christoffer Askman
88: Katie Boyette
89-90: Katie Bradley,
www.etsy.com/shop/MossyTortoise
91: Sarah Mundy, thesarahmundy.com
92: Patricia Waller, www.patriciawaller.com
93: Shove Mink, www.croshame.com
94-95: Stephanie Casper,
www.stephcasper.com
96-97: Trinlay Khadro,
www.zibbet.com/trinlayk /
www.flickr.com/photos/trinlayk
Character by Ophelia Chong, made with her
permission, www.flickr.com/opheliachong
sets/72157394331589705 /
www.opheliachong.org
98-99: Patricia Waller, www.patriciawaller.com
100: Travis F. Smith,
@nep on flickr unvarnished.com
101: Corrine Bayraktaroglu,
www.jafabrit.blogspot.com
102-103: Aletha Oberdier
104: Jessica Hendricks-McCullough
105: Ashley Gerst, www.ashleygerst.com
106-107: Katie Bradley,
www.etsy.com/shop/MossyTortoise
108-109: Nanae Ito,
www.iheartamicute.blogspot.fr

# About the authors

Gabrielle Grillo lives in Bordeaux, France, and she likes to knit conventional stuff like scarves and cardigans. She discovered the world of strange knits in 2010 and chose to start a Tumblr about it.

Lucy Sweet is a writer and cartoonist who lives in Glasgow, Scotland. She contributes to websites and publications such as the *Mirror*, Parentdish, Nickmom and *Glamour*. She has written two novels.

The authors would like to thank Susan Smith at MBA Literary Agency.